A11905 750284

DISCARD

DEMCO

Mankind

Pro Wrestler
Mick Foley

by Arlene Bourgeois Molzahn

Reading Consultant:
Dr. Robert Miller
Professor of Special Education
Minnesota State University, Mankato

CAPSTONE
HIGH-INTEREST
BOOKS

an imprint of Capstone Press
Mankato, Minnesota

Capstone High-Interest Books are published by Capstone Press
151 Good Counsel Drive, P.O. Box 669, Mankato, Minnesota 56002
http://www.capstone-press.com

Library of Congress Cataloging-in-Publication Data
Molzahn, Arlene Bourgeois.
   Mankind: pro wrestler Mick Foley/by Arlene Bourgeois Molzahn.
   p. cm.—(Pro wrestlers)
   Includes bibliographical references and index.
   Contents: A new champion—The early years—Becoming a wrestler—Professional
career—Mick Foley today.
   ISBN 0-7368-0919-8
   1. Foley, Mick—Juvenile literature. 2. Wrestlers—United States—Biography—
Juvenile literature. [1. Foley, Mick. 2. Wrestlers.] I. Title. II. Series
GV1196.F64 M65 2002
796.812'092—dc21
[B]   00-013074

Summary: Traces the personal life and career of professional wrestler Mick Foley.

Editorial Credits
Angela Kaelberer, editor; Lois Wallentine, product planning editor;
   Timothy Halldin, cover designer and illustrator; Katy Kudela, photo researcher

Photo Credits
Albert L. Ortega, 36
AP/Wide World Photos, 4, 7
Dr. Michael Lano, cover, cover inset (left), cover inset (right), 10, 13, 15, 16, 19, 20,
   23, 24, 27, 28, 40, 42
George De Sota/Liaison Agency, 33
PRNewsFoto, 34
Rich Freeda/WWF Entertainment/Liaison Agency, 30

1 2 3 4 5 6 07 06 05 04 03 02

Capstone Press thanks Dr. Michael Lano, WReaLano@aol.com, for his assistance in
the preparation of this book.

Table of Contents

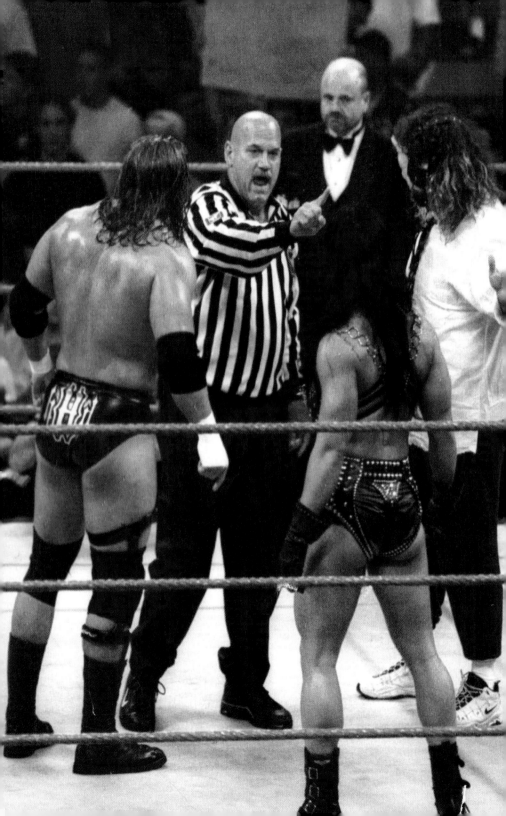

Chapter 1

A New Champion

It was August 22, 1999. Pro wrestling fans filled the Target Center in Minneapolis, Minnesota. They were there for SummerSlam. This event is one of the biggest in the World Wrestling Federation (WWF).

At SummerSlam, three wrestlers competed in a Triple Threat match for the WWF World Championship. These wrestlers were "Stone Cold" Steve Austin, Paul Levesque, and Mick Foley. Levesque is known as Hunter Hearst Helmsley or Triple H. Mick Foley was wrestling as Mankind. Austin was the current WWF World Champion.

Mick wrestled at SummerSlam 1999 with Minnesota Governor Jesse Ventura as the referee.

Minnesota Governor Jesse Ventura was the special referee for this match. Ventura wrestled for the WWF before he became governor.

Wrestler Joanie Laurer also was involved in the match. She is known as Chyna. Chyna was there to help Triple H.

Triple H and Austin began the match by punching each other. Mick pulled Triple H out of the ring. He slammed Triple H down on a table. Austin then threw Triple H onto the steel steps outside the ring.

The action continued both inside and outside of the ring. Chyna hit Mick and then pulled his legs between the ringpost. Ventura then made Chyna leave the ring.

Austin then used his signature move on Mick. This move is the Stone Cold Stunner. Austin wrapped his arm around Mick's head. Austin then dropped to his knees as he slammed Mick to the mat. Triple H then hit both Austin and Mick with a chair. Triple H tried to pin Mick. But Ventura would not count the pin.

Mick then performed his signature move. This move is the Mandible Claw. He grabbed Austin around the neck. He then pulled a sweat

"Stone Cold" Steve Austin was one of Mick's opponents at the SummerSlam match.

sock out of his pants. Mick called this sock "Mr. Socko." He stuffed the sock in Austin's mouth.

Austin knocked Mick away. He used the Stone Cold Stunner on Triple H. Mick stopped Austin from pinning Triple H. Triple H then tried to pin Austin. Mick punched Triple H to the mat. He gave Austin a double-arm DDT. Mick put a front facelock on Austin. He then fell straight down. Mick covered Austin for the pin as Ventura counted to three. Mick was the World Champion.

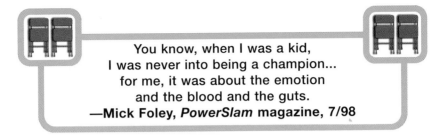

You know, when I was a kid,
I was never into being a champion...
for me, it was about the emotion
and the blood and the guts.
—Mick Foley, *PowerSlam* magazine, 7/98

About Mick Foley

Mick Foley began his career as a pro wrestler in 1986. He is 6 feet, 2 inches (188 centimeters) tall and weighs 287 pounds (130 kilograms). He often used the name Mankind when he wrestled. He also wrestled as Cactus Jack and Dude Love.

During the 1990s, Mick was one of the most popular wrestlers in the world. He wrestled for the WWF and World Championship Wrestling (WCW). He also wrestled for Extreme Championship Wrestling (ECW). During his career, Mick won the WWF World Championship three times and the WWF Tag Team Championship eight times.

Mick retired from wrestling in April 2000. But he still works for the WWF. He served as the WWF commissioner for about six months. In that job, he set up matches and sometimes served as an announcer or referee. Today, he often appears on the WWF's TV shows and at other WWF events.

8

Major Matches

May 22, 1994—As Cactus Jack, Mick teams with Kevin Sullivan to win the WCW Tag Team Championship.

July 14, 1997—As Dude Love, Mick teams with Steve Austin to win the WWF Tag Team Championship.

December 29, 1998—Mankind defeats The Rock to win his first WWF World Championship.

January 26, 1999—Mankind defeats The Rock to win his second WWF World Championship.

August 22, 1999—Mankind defeats Steve Austin and Triple H to win his third WWF World Championship.

August 30, 1999—Mankind and The Rock defeat the Undertaker and the Big Show for the WWF Tag Team Championship.

February 27, 2000—As Cactus Jack, Mick faces Triple H in a cage match; Mick loses the match and promises to retire.

April 2, 2000—Mick wrestles the final match of his career against Triple H, the Big Show, and The Rock.

Chapter 2

The Early Years

Michael Francis Foley was born June 7, 1965, in Bloomington, Indiana. His family called him Mick. Mick's parents are Beverly and Jack Foley. He has an older brother named John. The family moved to East Setauket, New York, when Mick and John were children.

The Foley family was involved in athletics. Jack was the athletic director for the East Setauket school system. Beverly was a physical education teacher at Setauket High School before she and Jack married.

Mick grew up in East Setauket, New York.

Jack took his sons to many sporting events. They went to football, basketball, and baseball games. They watched bowling, field hockey, and volleyball competitions. Mick and John also watched professional wrestlers on TV. Mick's favorite wrestler was Jimmy "Superfly" Snuka.

High School Athlete

Mick attended Ward Melville High School in East Setauket. In high school, he played basketball and football. But his best sport was lacrosse. In this game, players use long sticks attached to nets to catch, carry, and throw the ball. Mick played goalie for the team. His job was to keep the other team from throwing the ball into his team's net.

In 12th grade, Mick tried out for the wrestling team. He wanted to keep in shape to play lacrosse in the spring. Mick enjoyed wrestling and discovered that he was good at it. He lost interest in lacrosse.

Mick has wrestled since he was in high school.

Mick and his friends sometimes filmed their wrestling matches with a home movie camera. Later, they watched the movies and talked about their matches.

Mick and his friends also made some movies just for fun. Mick copied his hero Jimmy Snuka during one of these movies. He leaped off the roof of a two-story house and landed on a pile of old mattresses. This stunt was very dangerous. Mick was lucky that he was not hurt.

In June 1983, Mick watched Snuka wrestle Don Muraco at Madison Square Garden in New York City. Mick became even more interested in professional wrestling after this match.

Mick graduated from high school in 1983. Two colleges in Maryland offered him athletic scholarships to play lacrosse. These schools were Salisbury State University and Western Maryland College. But Mick turned down both scholarships. He had decided to become a professional wrestler.

Jimmy "Superfly" Snuka was Mick's favorite wrestler when Mick was growing up.

Snuka is 6 feet (183 centimeters) tall and wrestled at a weight of 250 pounds (113 kilograms). His real name is James Reiher.

During the 1980s, Snuka was one of the WWF's top wrestlers. His signature move was the bodysplash. Snuka later wrestled for Extreme Championship Wrestling (ECW). In 1991, he won two ECW World Championships.

In the early 1990s, Mick wrestled Snuka in Las Vegas, Nevada. The match ended in a double count-out. Mick and Snuka both jumped out of the ring and wrestled in the stands. Neither wrestler made it back into the ring before the referee counted to 10.

Chapter 3

Becoming a Wrestler

Mick wanted a career as a professional wrestler. But his parents wanted him to attend college. In fall 1983, he enrolled at State University of New York in Cortland, New York. This school is known as SUNY-Cortland. Mick majored in communications. He studied radio and TV production.

In October, Mick went home for fall vacation. He was due back at school on Monday, October 17. But Jimmy Snuka again was wrestling Don Muraco that night in Madison Square Garden.

Mick wanted a career as a pro wrestler.

It wasn't that he [Snuka] just jumped off the cage, it was the fact that it touched a lot of people...I always want to get emotion from the fans.
—**Mick Foley, E!Online, 12/00**

Mick hitchhiked to New York City to see the match. He did not tell his parents.

The match was a cage match. The ring was enclosed inside a steel cage. Snuka ended the match by leaping off the cage onto Muraco. After the match, Mick was more determined than ever to become a pro wrestler.

A week later, Mick talked to his parents. They asked him if he had enjoyed the wrestling match. Mick was going to say that he was not there. But he decided to tell the truth. His parents then said that they had seen him on TV. He was sitting in the third row. They made Mick promise that he would finish college before becoming a pro wrestler.

Training for a Dream
In 1985, a wrestling show came to Mick's old high school. At the match, Mick's father introduced him to wrestling promoter Tommy Dee. Dee organized wrestling shows. Dee

Mick has wrestled in cage matches like his hero Jimmy Snuka did.

watched the film of Mick jumping off the roof
of a house. Dee was impressed with Mick's feat.
He hired Mick to work as part of his ring crew.
Mick would help to set up the ring at Dee's
wrestling matches for $25 per match. Dee
promised that some of his wrestlers would help
Mick train to be a wrestler.

At a match, Mick met wrestler Dominic
DeNucci. DeNucci ran a school for wrestlers

During his career, Mick became friends with other wrestlers such as Owen Hart.

and set up matches for them. He agreed to train Mick. But DeNucci's school was in Freedom, Pennsylvania. This city was about 400 miles (640 kilometers) from Mick's college in Cortland. Every Friday night, Mick drove eight hours to Freedom. He slept in the back seat of his car until the gym opened. To save money, he ate only peanut butter sandwiches. He trained all weekend. On Sunday night, he drove back to Cortland.

Mick learned more than wrestling moves at DeNucci's school. He learned that wrestlers play a role during their matches. Some wrestlers act mean to their opponents and the fans. They are called "heels." Other wrestlers are heroes. They are called "babyfaces" or "faces."

Cactus Jack

On June 24, 1986, Mick wrestled his first match. The match took place in Clarksburg, West Virginia. Mick's opponent was Kurt Kaufman. Mick called himself Cactus Jack Manson. Cactus Jack was Mick's nickname for his father. Mick's character was a heel. Mick lost this match. But he kept training during the rest of the summer.

In August, DeNucci offered Mick the chance to wrestle at two WWF matches. The matches would be shown on TV.

Mick drove to Providence, Rhode Island, for the first match. About 18,000 fans filled the Providence Civic Center. Mick was Les Thornton's partner in a tag team match. Their opponents were David Smith and Tom

Billington. This team was known as the British Bulldogs. The British Bulldogs were the WWF Tag Team Champions. During the match, Mick took a hard punch in the jaw before falling to the mat. The Bulldogs won the match.

The second match was in Hartford, Connecticut. Mick's partner for this match was Terry Gibbs. They wrestled against Jim Brunzell and B. Brian Blair. These wrestlers were known as the Killer Bees. Mick and his partner lost the match. Mick's front teeth also were knocked loose. But he was starting to become known in the wrestling business.

Mick wrestled in several matches during his last year of college. Some of these matches were in high school gyms. He sometimes earned only $10 each night.

Mick worked hard to balance the demands of wrestling and his college classes. Mick did so well in school that he received the Anne Allen award. SUNY-Cortland gives this award each year to its top communications student. Mick graduated from college in 1987.

Mick wrestled some early matches in high school gyms.

Chapter 4

Professional Career

For a short time, Mick wrestled as Cactus Jack Manson. But he soon shortened this name to Cactus Jack. He used that name for nearly every match from 1986 to 1996.

Most wrestlers create a character that they use when they wrestle. They often wear a costume as part of the character. As Cactus Jack, Mick often wore a plaid shirt and cowboy boots. He pointed his fingers as if they were guns. He said, "Bang, bang," as he pretended to shoot the guns into the crowd.

As Cactus Jack, Mick pointed his fingers as if they were guns.

During Mick's early career, he wrestled as an independent. He did not work for a wrestling organization. Later, he worked for the Championship Wrestling Association (CWA) in Memphis, Tennessee. Mick also worked for World Class Championship Wrestling (WCCW) in Dallas, Texas.

In 1989, Mick joined the WCW. But he left the company in June 1990. The WCW's managers thought that Mick was taking too many chances when he wrestled. They told him that he would be seriously injured unless he changed his style of wrestling. Mick did not want to change. He went back to wrestling as an independent.

WCW Career

In 1989, Mick met Colette Christie at a racetrack in Long Island, New York. Colette was a model. In 1990, Mick and Colette married. Mick wanted to make more money to support his family. In 1991, he joined the WCW again. He spent the next three years wrestling for the WCW. He still wrestled as

Mick and Colette have been married since 1990.

Cactus Jack. But he now was a babyface
instead of a heel.

In 1994, Mick had several major injuries.
He wanted to take some time off to recover.
The WCW's managers wanted Mick to
continue wrestling. Mick again left the WCW
to wrestle as an independent. During the next
two years, Mick also wrestled many matches
for Extreme Championship Wrestling (ECW).

As Mankind, Mick wore a leather mask.

This organization was based in Philadelphia, Pennsylvania.

WWF and Mankind

Vince McMahon owns the WWF. In late 1995, McMahon asked Mick to wrestle for the WWF. But he did not want Mick to wrestle as Cactus Jack. McMahon told Mick that he would need to create a new character. Mick joined the WWF as Mankind in 1996.

As Mankind, Mick wore a leather mask and a white shirt. He wore a tie around his neck. He kicked and punched his way through matches. He used tables and chairs against his opponents. His favorite saying was, "Have a nice day." Mankind was supposed to be a heel. But he soon won the support of the fans. They began to cheer for him. He became a babyface.

As Mankind, Mick developed the Mandible Claw and Mr. Socko. After a match, Mick usually threw Mr. Socko into the crowd for a fan to catch.

Dude Love and Cactus Jack

In 1997, Mick created a character called Dude Love. Dude Love wore a fringed tie-dyed shirt. He wore mirrored sunglasses and a bandanna on his head. He danced to disco music as he entered the ring. Dude Love sometimes removed his shirt to show the crowd a red painted heart on his chest.

In September 1997, Mick wrestled as Cactus Jack at a match in Madison Square Garden. Mick's opponent was Triple H. Mick used a piledriver to put Triple H through a table

Rival in the Ring: Triple H

During Mick's later career, he wrestled many matches against Hunter Hearst Helmsley. These matches included his last three as a professional wrestler.

Helmsley also is known as Triple H. His real name is Paul Levesque. He is 6 feet, 4 inches (193 centimeters) tall and weighs 260 pounds (118 kilograms). His signature move is called the Pedigree. For this move, Triple H holds his opponent face down by the arms. The opponent's head is between his legs. He then drops to his knees as he slams the opponent's head into the mat.

Triple H began wrestling in 1992 as Terra Ryzing. In 1994, he joined the WCW. In the WCW, Triple H wrestled as Jean-Paul Levesque. In 1995, he joined the WWF. Triple H has won the WWF World Championship four times and the WWF Intercontinental Championship four times.

and win the match. During 1998, no one knew which character would show up during Mick's matches.

Mick's Later Career

Mick was successful during his years with the WWF. He won the WWF World Championship three times. He defeated The Rock in December 1998 and January 1999. In August 1999, he defeated Steve Austin and Triple H in a Triple Threat match. Mick then became a three-time WWF World Champion.

Mick also won the WWF Tag Team Championship four times in 1999. He won one of these titles with Al Snow. He teamed with The Rock to win the other three titles. Their team was called The Rock and Sock Connection.

In 2000, Mick decided to retire from wrestling. But he wanted his career to end with some exciting matches. Mick wrestled as Cactus Jack for two matches in early 2000. He faced Triple H during both matches. At the time, Triple H was the WWF World Champion.

Cactus Jack's Final Matches

The first match was at Madison Square Garden on January 23. Both wrestlers used weapons during this match. These weapons included a trash can, a board covered with wire, and thumbtacks. Mick used a piledriver to put Triple H through the announcer's table. But Triple H got up and performed two Pedigrees on Mick for the win.

The second match took place on February 27 in Hartford, Connecticut. Before the match, Mick promised that he would retire from wrestling if he lost.

During the match, the ring was completely enclosed in a metal cage. Both wrestlers battled inside and outside of the cage. They both climbed to the top of the cage. Triple H picked up Mick and threw him down on the cage. Mick fell through the cage and the ring. He left a large hole in the middle of the ring. Triple H then climbed off the cage into the ring. He gave Mick a Pedigree and then pinned him.

Triple H was Mick's opponent during Mick's last three matches.

After the match, ambulance workers were ready to load Mick onto a stretcher. But he refused. He walked out of the ring as the crowd cheered and chanted, "Foley, Foley." Mick then said that Cactus Jack, Mankind, and Dude Love would never wrestle for the WWF again.

Mick's career was not yet over. On April 2, 2000, he competed as himself at WrestleMania 16 in Anaheim, California. The match was a four-way elimination match. Mick's opponents were The Rock, Triple H, and Paul Wight. Wight wrestles as the Big Show.

Early in the match, Mick worked with The Rock and Triple H to eliminate the Big Show. The other three wrestlers continued the match until Triple H hit Mick with a chair. He then performed a Pedigree to pin Mick and eliminate him from the match. Triple H then eliminated The Rock to win the match and keep the World Championship.

Mick had hoped to retire as the World Champion. But he was happy to end his career at a big match against such great opponents.

Mick wrestled the Big Show during a number of WWF matches.

Chapter 5

Mick Foley Today

Mick retired from wrestling competition in April 2000. But he has not retired from the world of wrestling. He still works for the WWF.

Mick's Family

Mick and Colette live in Navarre, Florida, with their three children. Their sons' names are Dewey and Mickey. Their daughter is Noelle. Mick's family was one of the reasons that he retired. Wrestling required Mick to travel about 250 days each year. He missed spending time with his family. Mick also worried that

Mick wrote his autobiography in 1999.

wrestling's violence would have a bad effect on his children. Colette and the children became upset when Mick was hurt during his matches.

Mick now spends a great deal of time with his family. He often reads with his children and takes them to amusement parks.

A Favorite Holiday

Mick's favorite holiday is Christmas. He listens to Christmas music throughout the year. He keeps a toy Christmas village set up all year in his home. Santa's Christmas Village in New Hampshire was Mick's favorite childhood place to visit. Today, he takes his children to this amusement park.

In 2000, Mick decided to share his love of Christmas with children everywhere. He wrote a children's book called *Mick Foley's Christmas Chaos*. The story is about professional wrestlers who go to the North Pole to help Santa Claus. Professional wrestler and announcer Jerry Lawler drew the pictures for the book.

Mick's Injuries

During his career, Mick was known as one of the most physical pro wrestlers. He suffered many injuries while wrestling. He had eight concussions. These brain injuries usually are caused by a hard blow to the head. He broke his nose, jaw, wrist, cheekbone, and five ribs. He also received more than 300 stitches.

One of Mick's worst injuries occurred in 1994. At the time, Mick's main rival was WCW Champion Leon White. White wrestled as Vader.

On March 17, 1994, Mick wrestled Vader in Munich, Germany. During the match, Mick tried to perform a hangman. For this move, Mick crashed into the ropes. He then put his head between the second and third ropes as he flipped over and out of the ring.

Mick's head became caught between the ropes. He began to choke. As he struggled, the ropes ripped off part of his right ear. Mick continued to wrestle for another two minutes before Vader pinned him. Mick still is missing three-fourths of his right ear.

In 1999, Mick appeared in the movie *Beyond the Mat*.

Mick wrote the book after meeting a 4-year-old boy who had been badly burned. Mick wrote about the little boy in the book. He also gives part of the money he makes from the book to the Shriners Hospitals. These hospitals offer free treatment to children who are sick or hurt.

Author and Actor

In 1999, Mick wrote his autobiography. The book is called *Mankind, Have a Nice Day: A Tale of Blood and Sweatsocks*. Many famous people who write books about their lives hire professional writers to help them. But Mick wrote his book himself. He wrote the book by hand in a notebook because he does not own a computer or typewriter. The book was successful. It reached number one on the *New York Times* bestseller list.

Mick also has done some acting. He appeared on the TV shows *Now and Again, Saturday Night Live*, and *Boy Meets World*. Mick also appeared in a documentary movie about wrestling. This true story is called *Beyond the Mat*. Mick may act and write more books in the future. But he still plans to stay involved in wrestling.

Career Highlights

1965 — Mick is born June 7 in Bloomington, Indiana.

1986 — On June 24, Mick wrestles his first professional match as Cactus Jack Manson.

1987 — Mick graduates from SUNY-Cortland with a degree in communications.

1989 — Mick joins the WCW as Cactus Jack.

1996 — Mick joins the WWF as Mankind.

1997 — Dude Love and Steve Austin win the WWF Tag Team title.

1998 — Mick wrestles as Mankind to win the WWF World Championship and two Tag Team titles during the year; he also wins a Tag Team title as Cactus Jack.

1999 — Mick wrestles as Mankind to win his second and third WWF World Championships and four Tag Team Championships during the year; he also writes his autobiography.

2000 — Mick retires from professional wrestling and becomes the WWF commissioner; he also writes a children's book.

Words to Know

autobiography (aw-toh-bye-OG-ruh-fee)—a book in which the author tells the story of his or her life

commissioner (kuh-MISH-uh-nur)—a person who is in charge of a professional sport

concussion (kuhn-KUSH-uhn)—an injury to the brain caused by a hard blow to the head

documentary (dok-yuh-MEN-tuh-ree)—a movie or TV program about real situations and people

lacrosse (luh-KRAWSS)—a game in which players use long sticks attached to nets to catch, carry, and throw the ball

opponent (uh-POH-nuhnt)—a person who competes against another person

promoter (pruh-MOH-tur)—a person who organizes events such as concerts and wrestling matches

signature move (SIG-nuh-chur MOOV)—the move for which a wrestler is best known; this move also is called a finishing move.

44

To Learn More

Burgan, Michael. *The Rock: Pro Wrestler Rocky Maivia.* Pro Wrestlers. Mankato, Minn.: Capstone High-Interest Books, 2002.

Greenberg, Keith Elliot. *Pro Wrestling: From Carnivals to Cable TV.* Minneapolis: Lerner, 2000.

Ross, Dan. *Pro Wrestling's Greatest Wars.* Pro Wrestling Legends. Philadelphia: Chelsea House, 2001.

West, Terry M. *Mick Foley: Behind the Mankind Mask.* New York: Scholastic, 2000.

Useful Addresses

Extreme Canadian Championship Wrestling
211 20701 Langley Bypass
Langley, BC V3A 5E8
Canada

World of Wrestling Magazine
Box 500
Missouri City, TX 77459-9904

World Wrestling Federation Entertainment, Inc.
1241 East Main Street
Stamford, CT 06902

Internet Sites

Canadian Pro Wrestling Hall of Fame
http://www.canoe.ca/SlamWrestling/
   hallofame.html

Mick Foley.com
http://www.mickfoley.com/commish/
   index.html

Professional Wrestling Online Museum
http://www.wrestlingmuseum.com/home.html

WWF.com
http://www.wwf.com

Index